GRADE 5 FIVE
POWERTHINK
Cooperative Critical Thinking Activities

Written by Cindy Barden

Illustrated by Gary Mohrmann

Editor: Hanna Otero

Cover Design: Kristin Lock

Graphic Artists: Danielle Dela Cruz and Anthony Strasburger

Note on reproduction of this material: No part of this publication may be reproduced, stored in a retrieval system, or transmitted, in any form or by any means—electronic, mechanical, recording, or otherwise—without prior permission of the publisher. Reproduction of workbook activity pages by classroom teacher for use in the classroom and not for commercial sale is permissible. Reproduction of these materials for an entire school system is strictly forbidden.

FS112114 POWERTHINK–Grade Five
All rights reserved-Printed in the U.S.A.
Copyright ©2000 Frank Schaffer Publications
23740 Hawthorne Blvd., Torrance, CA 90505

Table of Contents

Introduction 4
POWERTHINKING 5
Think about Thinking 6
Non-Content Activities 7-18
    Brick Work 7
    Oh Say, Can You See? 8
    Carrots Make Your Ears Grow 9
    The Dictionary Habit 10
    Say What? 11
    Look for Yourself 12
    Can Your Senses Be Fooled? 13
    Think So Hard Your Head Explodes 14
    Where the Circles Meet 15
    Pocket Change 16
    What's the Connection? 17
    Somebody or Nobody? 18
Language Arts Activities 19-28
    Are You Like Tom Sawyer? 19
    An Everyday Poem 20
    What's the Rest of the Story? 21
    Ideas Popping like Popcorn 22
    How Convincing Are You? 23
    The Mystery of the Missing Title 24
    And Then What Happened? 25
    The Choice is Yours 26
    Design a Superhero 27-28
Social Studies Activities 29-37
    Do You Buy It? 29
    Plan Before You Start 30
    Day or Night Jobs? 31-32
    What if Green Was Illegal? 33
    Good Idea 34
    School Twelve Months a Year 35
    Help Wanted 36
    Sidewalk Planner 37

Mathematics Activities 38-44
    Circle, Rectangle, or Triangle? 38
    Jokers Aren't Wild 39
    Number Sleuth 40
    Best Buy 41
    Missing Pieces 42
    Too Good to Be True 43-44
Science Activities 45-51
    What the World Really Needs Is 45
    This Is Not a Test 46
    Why Do Zebras Have Stripes? 47
    More Questions 48
    A Robot for You 49
    Interplanetary Message 50
    The Shadow Knows 51
Art Activities 52-54
    Creating New Colors 52
    Reasons to Celebrate 53
    A Letter Without Words 54
Problem Solving Activities 55-61
    What's the Problem? 55
    What Next? 56
    Consider Your Choices 57
    What Would You Do? 58-59
    A Plan for Your Future 60
    Recognizing Feelings 61
Encouraging POWERTHINKING 62
Bibliography 63
Answers 64

INTRODUCTION

"There are one-story intellects, two-story intellects and three-story intellects with skylights. All fact collectors who have no aim beyond their facts are one-story people. Two-story people compare, reason, generalize, using the labor of the fact collectors as their own. Three-story people idealize, imagine, predict – their best illumination comes from above through the skylight."

Oliver Wendell Holmes

As educators, our goal is to assist students to become "third-story thinkers." Both the National Council of Teachers of Mathematics and the National Science Teachers Association recommend including problem solving and decision making as major goals of education.

What is critical thinking? Research indicates that the skill most basic to critical thinking is the ability to listen or read actively while continuously analyzing the information being presented. Sounds pretty basic, doesn't it? This ability requires the learner to be able to engage in an internal dialogue. Effective learners can dialogue internally without skipping steps.

Current recommendations suggest that children can best learn critical thinking skills by working in small groups or pairs. Working in pairs forces students to externalize their thinking – to think aloud, and to identify errors and skipped steps. It also teaches students to recognize and edit unsystematic thinking in themselves and others.

The **POWERTHINK** series of reproducible activity sheets is designed to provide cooperative learning opportunities for either small groups or pairs. There are six levels of challenge in the **POWERTHINK** series, allowing you to introduce critical thinking material at a sequential pace.

POWERTHINK has provided you with activity sheets that pertain to the major content areas of language arts, social studies, mathematics, science, art, and problem solving.

The **POWERTHINK** activity books have been designed to provide practice in:

Evaluating Information
Differentiating Between Fact and Opinion
Looking at Both Sides of an Issue
Solving Problems
Making Decisions
Observation
Synthesis
Searching for Alternative Solutions
Exploring New Ideas
Identifying and Clarifying
Setting Goals
Deductive Reasoning
Pre-planning
Giving and Following Directions
Comparing and Contrasting
Brainstorming
Predicting
Organizing Material

Because the teaching of critical thinking skills can also be a forum for truly individual positive reinforcement, on page 63 you will find a list of powerful verbal reinforcers. Use these to encourage your students as they become "**POWERTHINKERS.**"

Happy **POWERTHINKING!**

POWERTHINKING

What is **THINKING?**

Thinking can be many things. To see that this is true, try this:

DON'T THINK! Close your eyes for one minute and do not think of anything at all.

Did it work? Did you find yourself thinking about something? Or thinking about how you weren't supposed to be thinking?

So, where and when do you think? In school, of course. That's obvious. But if you're thinking all the time, there must be other times and places for thinking. You are also thinking when you...

- read a magazine
- decide which television program to watch
- climb a tree
- go for a walk in the country
- write a letter
- play a video game
- go on a vacation with your family
- listen to your grandparents tell about "the old days"
- lie on your back and look at the clouds
- get into an argument

Remember: there are many ways to think. And you're thinking all the time.

Now, what is **POWERTHINKING?**

The power of thinking is greater than all other kinds of power combined! Think about the person who discovered that a wheel made it a lot easier to move a big rock. That person's brainpower was stronger than a whole team of big, muscular rock movers. You can use **POWERTHINKING** to solve problems that are too big for any other type of power!

Can you remember a time when you used thinking to solve a problem, make a really tough decision, or get out of a jam? Thinking gives you POWER. Power to turn a bad situation into a good one, to turn a defeat into a victory, and even to make someone with hurt feelings feel better. There is no limit to your thinking power. And, there are lots of ways to make your thinking even more powerful than it already is!

Every page in your **POWERTHINK** book will have a little area called "**LIGHTNING STRIKES**." This is the place for you to write down whatever flashes into your mind as you're doing the activity on the page. Like real lightning strikes, these stray thoughts come and go in a split second. So when you have a lightning strike, write it down quickly, before you forget it. Some of these strikes are going to be pretty wacky. But write them all down anyway. You can always cross out the sillier lightning strikes later, or transfer them to a silly thoughts file. But maybe, just maybe, that nutty idea will lead you to think about a problem in a new way. The lightning strike may not be the answer you want, but it may lead you to the answer you are looking for. So remember: write down whatever is on your mind. Try it! You'll be amazed at the powerful stuff that flashes around in your brain.

Each activity in your **POWERTHINK** book also includes a "**POWER PLAY**." POWER PLAYS are questions that will challenge you and take you and your powerful thinking machine one step further.

POWERTHINKING asks you to look at your mind as a muscle. The more you use it, the stronger it gets. If you keep using it, keep stretching it, before long, you'll be thinking with real power. That's what **POWERTHINKING** is all about: learning to use and strengthen your mind. You will find that you can use **POWERTHINKING** at school, but you will also use it at home, during vacations, and for the rest of your life!

Name(s)_____

THINK ABOUT THINKING

What is thinking?
　　How do you think?
　　　　Why do you think?
　　　　　　When do you think?
　　　　　　　　What do you think about?
　　　　　　　　　　Where is the best place to think?
　　　　　　　　　　　　What are the qualities of a good thinker?
　　　　　　　　　　　Do you need silence to think?

Work with a partner to list as many things as you can about thinking. Write down words and phrases that come to mind. Don't worry about using complete sentences.

Draw a picture of your ideal thinking place.

Write down a problem you'd like to think about.

_____

Describe how you think when you…

a. play chess.
b. solve a math problem.
c. write a letter.
d. build a treehouse.
e. watch a baseball game.
f. read the newspaper.
g. listen to music.

_____
_____
_____
_____

POWER PLAY

When you don't have anything important to think about, think about thinking - on the bus, walking to school, as you fall asleep at night.

LIGHTNING STRIKES

6　Frank Schaffer Publications　　　　　　　　　　　　　　　　　　　　FS112114 POWERTHINK

Name(s)_____

BRICK WORK

"Most people would rather die than think ... and most do!"
—Bertrand Russel, British Philosopher

You exercise your body to improve your muscles. Your brain needs exercise too. Here are some stretching exercises for your brain. Work with a partner because exercising together is more fun than exercising alone.

The Situation: You and your partner are the research team for Bricks Unlimited, a student-run brick company. Bricks Unlimited has sold bricks to builders for many years. But now the company wants to sell bricks to other people as well. Your job is to come up with new uses for a brick.

Describe each new use with a couple of sentences and then draw a diagram. Stretch your mind to go beyond the ordinary, everyday uses for bricks.

After you and your partner have come up with some ideas, pick the best one. Make up an advertisement to sell your brick product to the public. Include an illustration, selling points, the price, and anything else you think is needed to sell your new idea.

POWER PLAY

Looking at an ordinary object in a new way can be good exercise for your brain. Walk around the house or classroom. What do you see? What other uses could you find for these objects?

Challenge your family to exercise with you to think of new uses for a ping pong ball, a bar of soap, or a wooden spoon.

NEW!
Industrial Grade DOOR STOP
Only $4.95!

Impervious to flame, water, wind and noxious fumes! Will not rot or rust! Stops even the heaviest door!

LIGHTNING STRIKES

Now, what if the bricks were 100 times larger than a normal brick? What are some possible uses for the giant brick? List ideas, pick the best one, and make up an advertisement.

FS112114 POWERTHINK

Frank Schaffer Publications

7

Name(s)_____

OH SAY, CAN YOU SEE?

Read the words in the triangle. Write the words that you read:

```
     ROME
    IN THE
   THE WINTER
```

_____

How many words did you write? If you wrote five words, good for you. You're very observant. If you wrote four words, go back to the triangle and look again. Did you find the fifth word?

Sometimes we see what we expect to see rather than what is really present.

Part of being a critical thinker is being observant. Without looking, what color socks are you wearing?

You look at things everyday, but do you really SEE them?

How many sides does a stop sign have?

Which shoe do you put on first, your right or your left?

Without looking, which of your classmates wear glasses?

Which ones have blond hair?

What items are on your dresser at home?

Is red at the top or bottom of a stop light?

What color are the curtains in your kitchen?

How many windows are there in your front room?

Which arm do you put in first when you put your jacket on?

POWER PLAY

How many things do you look at, but not see?

How can being more observant help you be a POWERTHINKER?

LIGHTNING STRIKES

Name(s)_____

CARROTS MAKE YOUR EARS GROW

A **claim** is a statement that is true or false.

   The temperature is 63 degrees right now.

   Franklin is nine feet, three inches tall.

   Eating carrots makes your ears grow longer.

Not every sentence is a claim. Here are some examples that are not claims.

   Where are you going?   (a question)
   Hello.   (a greeting)
   Shut off the light.   (an order)
   Let's play tennis today.   (a suggestion)

Read each sentence below. If it is a claim, put a C in the space after the sentence. If it is not a claim, put an N in the space after the sentence. Do not worry if the claim is true or false.

1. Josh likes pizza more than he likes lima beans. _____
2. Boston is the capital of New York. _____
3. Would you like liver and onions for supper? _____
4. Iceberg Cereal tastes better than sawdust. _____
5. Eating spinach makes your eyes turn green. _____
6. Let's enter the mud wrestling match. _____
7. Hand me that walrus. _____
8. I can lift a piano with one hand. _____
9. Do you want to take bagpipe lessons? _____
10. Your purple hair looks terrific! _____

Check your answers. Did you recognize which statements were claims and which were not? Review any that you missed. See if you can spot where you went wrong.

Write three claims of your own. It doesn't matter if they are true or false.

_____
_____
_____

POWER PLAY

With your partner make your own list of sentences, similar to the ones found on this page. Only half of the sentences should be claims. The other sentences can be questions, greetings, orders and suggestions.

Give your list to another group of students and let them find the claims.

LIGHTNING STRIKES

Name(s)_____

THE DICTIONARY HABIT

Before you can check a fact, you need to understand the words in the statement. Same goes for opinions. Before you can decide whether or not to agree, you have to know what all the words mean.

Some statements contain words we may not know.

    Democracy is a better form of government than monarchy.

    His ostensible appearance made others dubious about his acquiescent attitude.

When statements contain words that are unfamiliar, you can look them up in a dictionary or other reference source. You can understand claims by replacing the words you don't know with the words you do.

Use a dictionary or other reference source to check the meaning of any words you don't understand in the statements below. Rewrite each claim.

1. Trepidation in the dentist's waiting room caused Lisa's heart to palpitate.

   _____
   _____

2. Troy's nascence made me dubious about the veracity of his dissertation on Africa.

   _____
   _____

3. A facsimile of the "Mona Lisa" was sold to a gullible art collector for $10 million by an unscrupulous art dealer.

   _____
   _____

POWER PLAY

With a partner, rewrite a familiar saying or quotation, substituting complex, little-known synonyms for some of the words. Read the new saying. Is it as effective or meaningful as the original quotation?

When might it be better to leave out a long, complicated word when a simpler one would do?

LIGHTNING STRIKES

Frank Schaffer Publications

FS112114 POWERTHINK

Name(s)_____

SAY WHAT?

Understanding all the words used in a statement is one part of being able to decide if it is a fact or an opinion. But understanding all the words in a statement may not be enough.

Some claims are poorly written or stated and the meaning is not clear.

> Kim knows a little Italian.

Does this mean that Kim knows a young person from Italy or that she knows a few words in the Italian language?

> Jaimie saw the lion with binoculars.

Is Jaimie looking through binoculars at a lion or is he looking at a lion who has binoculars?

Read each of the claims and think about why they are not clear. Work with a partner. Discuss why the claim is not clear. After each statement, write two possible meanings for each claim.

1. Mother gave Todd the salad dressing and he put it on himself.

   _____
   _____

2. Sara likes milkshakes more than Edward.

   _____
   _____

3. The biggest football fans live in small cities.

   _____
   _____

4. Tim followed the girl on his bicycle.

   _____
   _____

POWER PLAY

When you read or listen to people speak, watch closely for claims that are not clear. You can't decide if a statement is true or false if the meaning isn't clear.

LIGHTNING STRIKES

Name(s)_____

LOOK FOR YOURSELF

To **observe** means to look at or examine something closely. One way to check a fact is to observe.

If two facts conflict, both cannot be true. As a **POWERTHINKER** you can observe to judge whether one of the two facts is correct.

KILOWATT QUESTION
The dog is blue.
The dog is red.

Both statements cannot be true. You also know that dogs are not usually red or blue. How could you determine which claim, if either, is correct?

MEGAWATT QUESTION
The glass is filled with cold water.
The glass is filled with hot water.

These statements appear to conflict. However, there is a problem. We do not know exactly what we mean when we say "hot" or "cold."

Describe a situation where water that feels cold to one person might feel hot to another person.

Revise the two statements to turn them into conflicting facts that can be checked.

POWER PLAY
With a partner, write two conflicting facts.

Now describe how you could check them to determine which fact was true and which was false.

LIGHTNING STRIKES

---

12 Frank Schaffer Publications   FS112114 POWERTHINK

Name(s)_____

CAN YOUR SENSES BE FOOLED?

You rely on your senses of sight, taste, touch, hearing, and smell to make observations and help determine if a claim is true or false. But...

What if you have a head cold?

What if the sun is shining in your eyes?

What if someone is playing loud music?

What if your hands are cold?

Sometimes you cannot rely entirely on your senses.

Work with a partner to describe situations when your senses may not be reliable. What could you do about the situation?

Here's an example: If it was dark, I might not be able to tell the color of an object. I could turn on a light to see better.

POWER PLAY

Work with a partner to describe situations when your senses may not be reliable. What could you do about your situation?

List some extra senses you wouldn't mind having.

LIGHTNING STRIKES

THINK SO HARD YOUR HEAD EXPLODES

Using your senses is one way to determine the truth of claims. Facts you have learned from observation (rain is wet) and facts you have learned from other sources (12 inches equal one foot) also help you.

If someone said, "Michael Jordan is the president of the United States," you would know that claim is not true.

Live Dinosaurs Discovered in Miami
118 Pound Baby Boy Born in Baltimore
Cabbage Patch Doll Eats Iceberg Cereal

Look at each of the headlines above and think about why they are probably not true, based on what you have learned from other sources.

When you go to a supermarket or newsstand, read the headlines on the front pages of several papers. Do you have any reason to believe that some of these claims may not be true?

Now it's your turn to write some claims.

Write your claims below. Include some that are false.

1. _____
   _____
2. _____
   _____
3. _____
   _____

Trade papers with a partner. See if you can find the claims which are not true in each other's papers.

POWER PLAY

The more knowledge you have, the better you will be at telling true claims from false ones. The best way to become a better **POWERTHINKER** is to increase what you know.

OBSERVE • READ • LISTEN • ASK QUESTIONS

LIGHTNING STRIKES

Name(s)_____

WHERE THE CIRCLES MEET

One way of showing how two things are alike and how they are different is to use a Venn diagram. Similarities between the two items are written in the section where the two circles meet. Differences are written in the far right and left sides where the circles do not intersect.

Work with one or two partners to fill in the similarities and differences between flowers and trees.

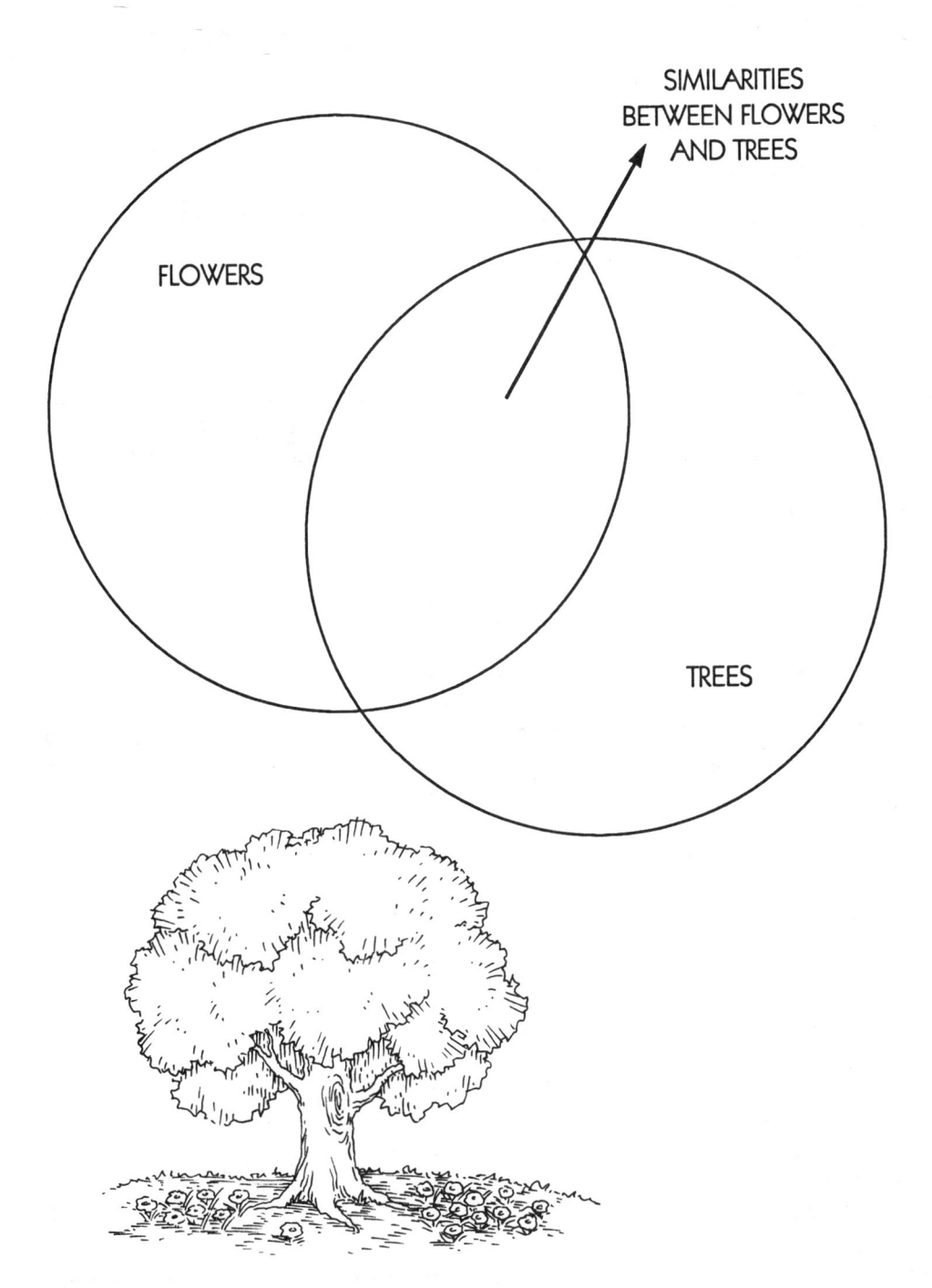

SIMILARITIES BETWEEN FLOWERS AND TREES

FLOWERS

TREES

POWER PLAY

How does a Venn diagram give you a visual picture of the similarities and differences between two items? Wouldn't this be a useful way to compare characters in a book, candidates running for office, chemicals, or scientific theories and ideas?

LIGHTNING STRIKES

FS112114 POWERTHINK

Frank Schaffer Publications

15

Name(s)_____

POCKET CHANGE

POWERTHINKERS look at a situation in several ways. They see not only the obvious, but other less-obvious possibilities.

Work with one or two classmates on this activity. How many captions can you come up with for the cartoon below? Write them below the cartoon.

POWER PLAY
With a partner, list at least 10 descriptions of what the object in the box might be.

LIGHTNING STRIKES

16 Frank Schaffer Publications

FS112114 POWERTHINK

Name(s)_____

WHAT'S THE CONNECTION?

Here's a new twist to a crossword puzzle. Instead of giving you direct clues to the words, the clues are three words that have something in common. If the clue was roses, daisies, and lilies, the answer would be flowers.

How about hopscotch, Monopoly, and baseball? What about Kennedy, Washington, and Lincoln? Find the common link and you'll have the word to fill in for the puzzle.

Hint: Sometimes items could have more than one thing in common. Turtles, frogs, and alligators are all animals. They are also reptiles. Use the word that fits the puzzle.

POWER PLAY

Now that you have finished the puzzle, you know what all the items in each clue have in common.

With your partner, consider those clues again. Try to think of how they are all different from each other.

LIGHTNING STRIKES

Across
1. Asia, North America, Europe
4. Sombrero, baseball, top
7. Falcons, cardinals, blue jays
9. Alaska, Arizona, Arkansas
14. Pacific, Atlantic, Indian
17. Bambi, Superman, Star Wars
18. 1948, 1964, 1917
19. Oregon, Chisholm, Mormon
20. Collies, greyhounds, pugs
21. Rattlers, cobras, boas

Down
1. Rome, Paris, New York
2. Creak, squeak, ring
3. Octagon, hexagon, circle
5. Tops, jacks, balls
6. Mississippi, Missouri, Colorado
8. Lions, tigers, Siamese
10. Bees, ants, termites
11. Martin Luther King, Jr. Day, Independence Day, Halloween
12. Cats, dogs, mice
13. Chocolate, mints, licorice
15. Baseball, golf, swimming
16. April, May, June

SOMEBODY OR NOBODY?

Mr. Nobody and Ms. Somebody plan to get married soon. There's one small problem stopping them from setting the date. Ms. Somebody wants to keep her last name after they get married. Mr. Nobody wants her to change it. He thinks she should be Mrs. Nobody. He wants their children to be little Nobodys.

Ms. Somebody likes her last name. She wants to stay a Somebody. If they have children, the girls could be Somebodys and the boys could be Nobodys. Mr. Nobody won't agree.

Ms. Somebody suggested they could use both names and be Mr. and Mrs. Somebody-Nobody. That idea didn't make Mr. Nobody happy either. If they don't find an answer to their problem soon, there won't be a wedding.

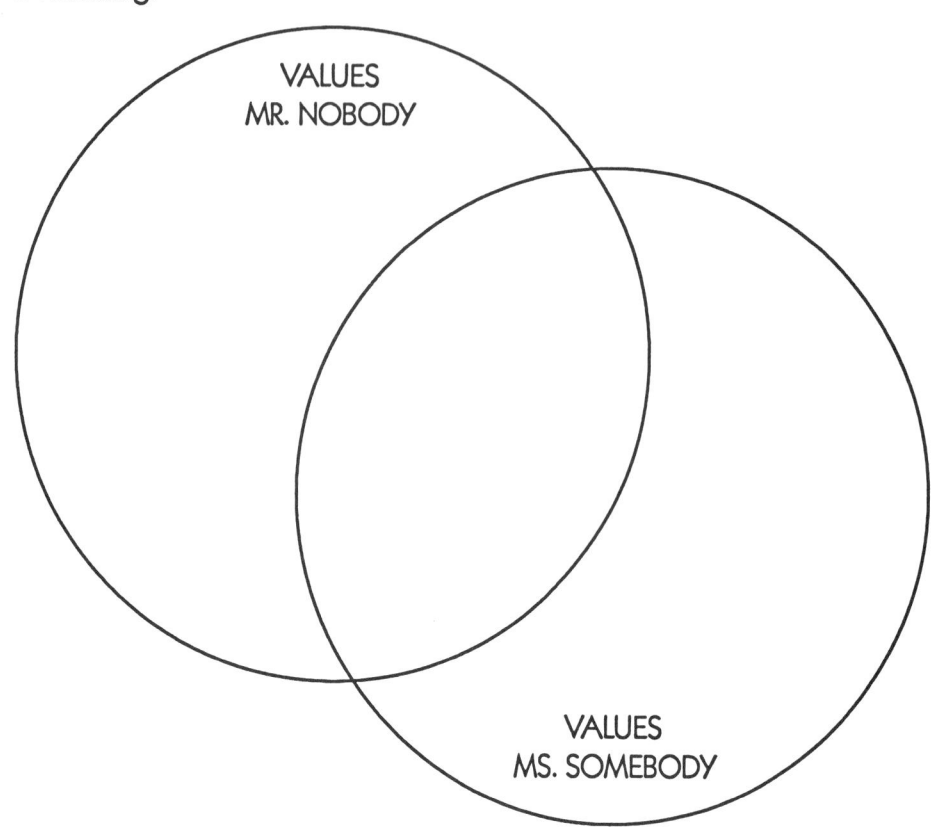

POWER PLAY

Work with a partner to choose something you'd like to see changed in your school. Use a Venn diagram to help find possible solutions to that problem.

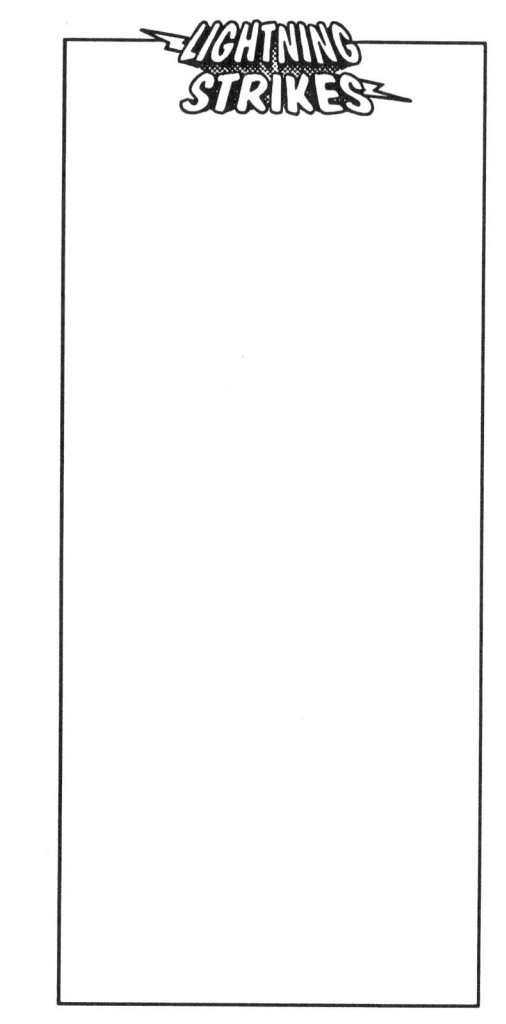

LIGHTNING STRIKES

(Venn diagram: VALUES MR. NOBODY / VALUES MS. SOMEBODY)

1. Think about the values that are important to Mr. Nobody and Ms. Somebody.
2. Fill in the Venn diagram to show which values are important to each person, and which values they share.
3. List all of the alternatives for Mr. Nobody and Ms. Somebody, including calling off the wedding.

What advice can you and your partner give Mr. Nobody and Ms. Somebody on their problem?

Name(s) _____

ARE YOU LIKE TOM SAWYER?

When you read, you may notice similarities between yourself and one of the characters. Maybe you've felt like Wart in the book *Wart, Son of Toad* or like Peter Hatcher in *Tales of a Fourth Grade Nothing*.

Select one of the main characters from a book or story. See how many ways you can find that you are like the character.

Name of book or story: _____

Name of character: _____

List ways that you and the character are alike.

_____
_____
_____

List ways that you and the character are different.

_____
_____
_____

Every character, like every person, has strengths and weaknesses. List some strengths you saw in the character that you also see in yourself.

_____
_____

Now list some weaknesses.

_____
_____

How did the character solve problems?

_____
_____

How do *you* solve problems?

_____
_____
_____
_____

POWER PLAY

How can comparing yourself with a character help you understand that character better? How could it help you understand yourself better?

LIGHTNING STRIKES

FS112114 POWERTHINK   Frank Schaffer Publications

Name(s)_____

AN EVERYDAY POEM

Some poets write about lofty ideas, gorgeous sunsets, or beautiful flowers. Poems can be about common things too. William Carlos Williams wrote a poem about a wheelbarrow.

What's the most common, ordinary, everyday thing you can think of? A sneeze? A shoe string? A piece of gravel? An empty soda can?

Here's an example of a free verse poem:

Lost Innocence
My tattered old sneakers
Once new,
Filled with wonder
Together we explored Spring.

1. Pick a common, everyday object.

2. As quickly as you can, write down words or phrases that the object brings to mind. Try to forget that you are in the process of writing a poem. Concentrate only on the object. Look at the object close up. Then look at the object from across the room. Stand on your head and look. Plug your ears and look.

3. After about five minutes of frantic writing, stop.

4. Use the words and phrases you wrote to make up a free-verse poem.

5. Share the poem with your friends and family.

POWER PLAY

Select your best poem. Rewrite it neatly on good paper. Illustrate it if you'd like. Ask your teacher to display the best poems written by everyone in the class.

LIGHTNING STRIKES

Frank Schaffer Publications

FS112114 POWERTHINK

Name(s)_____

WHAT'S THE REST OF THE STORY?

Some stories end too soon. They leave you wanting to know more about a character. What was Huck Finn like when he grew up? Did Tom Sawyer and Becky eventually get married? In *The Year of the Boar and Jackie Robinson*, did Mabel become a professional baseball player?

What character would you like to know more about?
_____

What are some questions about that character left unanswered at the end of the story? _____
_____
_____
_____
_____
_____

Answer your own questions. What do you think happened? What was that character like 10 years later?
_____
_____
_____
_____
_____
_____
_____

POWER PLAY

It's interesting to ask others what they think happened to a character after the story ended. Share your work with someone who has read the same story. Compare your answers to get even more ideas about the rest of the story.

LIGHTNING STRIKES

FS112114 POWERTHINK

Frank Schaffer Publications

21

Name(s)_____

IDEAS POPPING LIKE POPCORN

Writers often use **similes** to give readers a clear picture. A simile is a phrase that uses the words "like" or "as" to compare two items.

    Jessie was as hot as a fried egg on a griddle.
    His eyes were like storm clouds.

Finish each phrase by writing a simile.

The fish was as large as _____

The music sounded like _____

The rainbow was like _____

The pitcher threw like _____

Kevin ran as _____ as _____

Marty talked like _____

The show was as dull as _____

My friend is as smart as _____

The wind blew like _____

The rain sounded like _____

Ideas popped like _____

Dad roared like _____

Shirley hopped up and down like _____

Look at this _____. It's as _____

Write three similes of your own.

_____

_____

_____

POWER PLAY

As you read, watch for similes. How does the use of similes make a story more interesting? Write a short poem using at least one simile.

LIGHTNING STRIKES

Name(s) _____

HOW CONVINCING ARE YOU?

Are you a good salesperson? Could you sell an air conditioner in Antarctica? You'd have to be very convincing to do that.

What about selling a good book or story? Select a book or story you've read. Write a one-minute commercial to convince others to read it. Work with a partner to write and draw a storyboard for the commercial. A storyboard is a plan for matching words with pictures. Both of you could have parts to say or something to do in the commercial.

1. ☐
2. ☐
3. ☐
4. ☐

After you've written the commercial, perform it for the class. Did you get any buyers?

POWER PLAY

Advertising is a way to get others interested in a product, person, or idea.

You and your partner each create a storyboard for a commercial that is familiar to both of you. Try to remember as many words and pictures as possible. Don't look at one another's storyboards until you're finished!

Compare your storyboards. Did you both remember the same parts of the commercial? Talk about the parts of the commercial that were most convincing.

LIGHTNING STRIKES

FS112114 POWERTHINK

Frank Schaffer Publications

23

Name(s)_____

THE MYSTERY OF THE MISSING TITLE

Can you get your classmates to guess the title of a book or story without saying a word? Draw five items from a book or story that you've read. If you read *Charlotte's Web* you might draw a spider web as one of the clues. For *Charlie and the Chocolate Factory* you could draw a candy bar.

Draw the items on the covers of the books below.

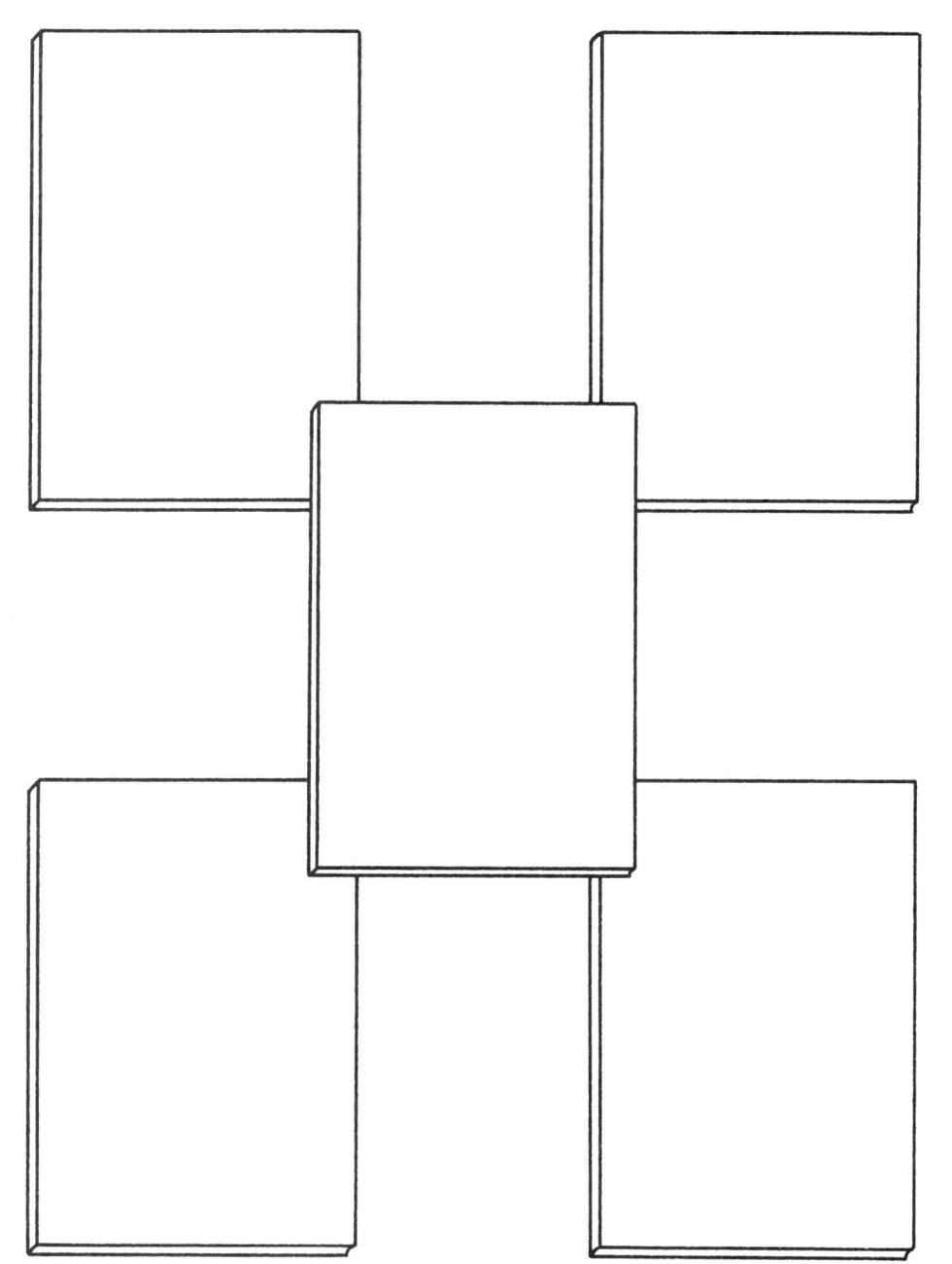

POWER PLAY

With a partner, draw several traffic signs. Use familiar signs or make up your own. For each sign, try to think of an actual book title that the sign could illustrate. Or, make up your own title.

LIGHTNING STRIKES

Show your drawing to classmates and see if they know what book or story you had in mind.

Name(s)_____

AND THEN WHAT HAPPENED? 25

Look at the first three panels in this cartoon. What do you think will happen in the final panel?

Draw the action and write the words needed to finish the cartoon. The ending can be humorous or serious.

Finish the cartoon by drawing in the final action and writing the words needed.

Panel 1: "It's almost time."
Panel 2: "I can hardly wait."
Panel 3: "I'm ready when you are."

There is no "right" ending. How does your ending differ from your classmates'? Display your cartoons on the bulletin board for everyone to enjoy.

POWER PLAY

With a partner, cut out one or two weeks' worth of a single comic strip. Don't use the Sunday funnies—just the black-and-white weekday strips. Cut out individual panels. Rearrange the panels to create a brand new, if slightly wacky, comic story. Share the story with your family and friends.

LIGHTNING STRIKES

Name(s)_____

THE CHOICE IS YOURS

Think about the **POWERTHINKING** skills you've learned. Apply them to complete one of the activities below.

Write a theme song for a novel.

Design a t-shirt encouraging people to read or featuring a favorite character or scene from a book.

Write a campaign slogan for a fictional character running for president.

Write a jingle to sell a book.

Keep a journal every day for two weeks. Write down your ideas, thoughts, and feelings.

Bring in a photograph. Write a story about the picture.

Compare and contrast the settings or characters from two stories.

Compare the best book you've ever read to the best meal you've ever eaten.

Analyze why a character acted the way he or she did in a specific situation. Think about how you would have reacted in the same situation.

What if books had headlines instead of titles? Write headlines for several books you've read.

POWER PLAY

List some specific situations where you could use one of the **POWERTHINKING** skills you've learned. Specify which thinking skill you would use and how it would apply to that situation.

LIGHTNING STRIKES

26
Frank Schaffer Publications
FS112114 POWERTHINK

Name(s)_____

DESIGN A SUPERHERO

It is the year 2034. A giant asteroid is streaking toward Earth. It looks like a job for Superman! Unfortunately, Superman is on vacation in Florida. So it's your job to use **POWERTHINKING** to design an all-new superhero to save the planet from the asteroid.

One way to **POWERTHINK** about a new superhero is to break the superhero down into parts, or categories. For example, here are a few categories:

Name, superpowers, costume, special equipment, hobbies, favorite food…

Try to think of several more. (To help you, think about how you would divide *yourself* into categories.)

Now that you've broken the superhero down into parts, describe each category by filling in this chart:

LIGHTNING STRIKES

Name:
Superpower #1
Superpower #2
Superpower #3
Costume
Special Equipment
Hobbies
Favorite Food

FS112114 POWERTHINK

Frank Schaffer Publications

Name(s)_____

DESIGN A SUPERHERO

Together with your partner, look over your superheroes.
Answer these questions:

Your Superhero   **Your Partner's Superhero**

Name _____   Name _____

1. Explain why superpowers 1, 2, and 3 will help your superhero destroy the asteroid.

   _____   _____
   _____   _____

2. How will the special equipment help your superhero destroy the asteroid?

   _____   _____
   _____   _____

3. Come up with three things that could go wrong as your superhero is trying to destroy the asteroid.

   _____   _____
   _____   _____
   _____   _____

4. Figure out ways your superhero could solve each of these problems.

   _____   _____
   _____   _____
   _____   _____

POWER PLAY

It wouldn't take long for your superhero to take care of a little asteroid problem. So what is he or she going to do to keep busy after the big job is done?

Brainstorm with your partner to think of everyday problems that Earth faces. Select one of the problems you thought of and tell how your superhero would solve this problem.

LIGHTNING STRIKES

Name(s)_____

DO YOU BUY IT?

Why do companies advertise? Talk about this with your partner and list several reasons.

_____
_____
_____

Advertisers use exciting music; gorgeous, smiling models; famous athletes; beautiful scenery; drama, and humor to sell products. The ads imply that you will be as beautiful or handsome as the models, as good at sports as the athletes, and your life will be happy and exciting as the lives of the people shown. Do ads create a false image of what life should be like?

Talk with your partner about some ads you've seen. List some specific ads and the means they use to convince people to buy products.

Ad: _____
Product: _____
Means of persuasion: _____
_____
_____

Ad: _____
Product: _____
Means of persuasion: _____
_____
_____

Ad: _____
Product: _____
Means of persuasion: _____
_____
_____

POWER PLAY

Some ads are vague, misleading, or even false. Some imply your life will be greatly improved if you buy their products. Be aware of the techniques used. When you page through a magazine or watch television, be conscious of how advertisers try to persuade people to buy their products.

LIGHTNING STRIKES

Name(s)_____

PLAN BEFORE YOU START

When you are asked to write a report about two people, places, things, experiences, or ideas, a good way to organize your material is by listing similarities and differences between the two.

Before you start comparing and contrasting, spend a few minutes thinking about the types of things you want to know.

If you were writing about two states, you might look for similarities and differences in climate, size, population, agriculture, and recreation.

List some other types of information you could compare and contrast about two states:

_____

_____

_____

What types of information would you want to compare if you had to write about two presidents?

_____

_____

_____

What if you were writing about two forms of government?

_____

_____

_____

How about two Native American tribes?

_____

_____

_____

POWER PLAY
Pre-planning can save you time on an assignment. Looking for similarities and differences can help you organize material.

LIGHTNING STRIKES

DAY OR NIGHT JOBS?

When people work day shift they may have trouble getting to doctor appointments or attending school functions held during the day.

When they work second shift (about 3 PM to 11 PM), they miss many prime-time TV shows, parties, and evening school functions.

People who work third shift (about 11 PM to 7 AM) need to sleep at unusual hours.

Each shift has advantages and disadvantages.

Work with a partner to think of advantages and disadvantages of working different shifts. Then think up three facts about working each shift that are interesting, but neither advantages nor disadvantages. Talk about your ideas. Work in any order you want and jump around as much as you like.

Three advantages of working first shift:

1. _____
2. _____
3. _____

Three disadvantages of working first shift:

1. _____
2. _____
3. _____

Three interesting facts about working first shift:

1. _____
2. _____
3. _____

Continue working on the advantages and disadvantages of different shifts on the next page.

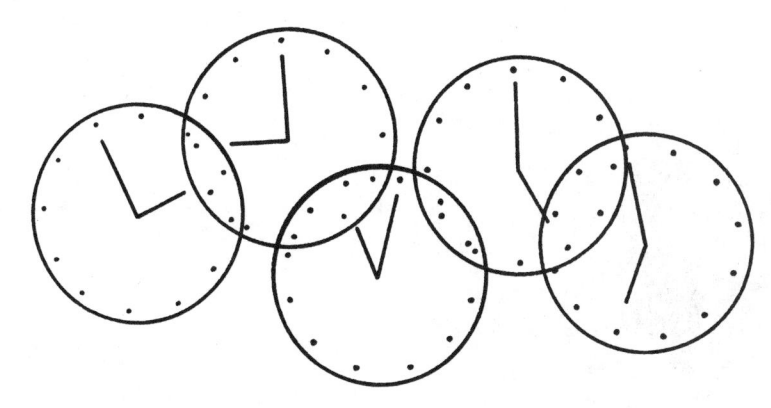

LIGHTNING STRIKES

Name(s)_____

DAY OR NIGHT JOBS?

Three advantages of working second shift are:

1. _____
2. _____
3. _____

Three disadvantages of working second shift are:

1. _____
2. _____
3. _____

Three interesting facts about working second shift:

1. _____
2. _____
3. _____

Three advantages of working third shift are:

1. _____
2. _____
3. _____

Three disadvantages of working third shift are:

1. _____
2. _____
3. _____

Three interesting facts about working third shift:

1. _____
2. _____
3. _____

POWER PLAY

Hospitals need people on duty 24 hours a day. Police officers and fire fighters must always be available. What are some other occupations that require people to work second and third shift? What shift would you like to work?

LIGHTNING STRIKES

Frank Schaffer Publications

FS112114 POWERTHINK

Name(s)_____

WHAT IF GREEN WAS ILLEGAL?

Have you ever sat around with a group of people talking about what to do, where to go, or who to vote for in the class election? If you have, you've already done some brainstorming, because that's what brainstorming is all about - getting together in a group and sharing your thoughts by thinking out loud.

Work in a small group. Select one of the topics below and start brainstorming. One person should write down ALL ideas - good or bad, silly or practical. Don't worry about complete sentences. Use the back of this sheet to record your ideas.

1. What are some alternatives for latch key kids (kids who go home after school to an empty house or apartment because parents work)?
   _____
   _____

2. What if the color green was illegal?
   _____
   _____

3. How would people react if friendly aliens landed on Earth?
   _____
   _____

4. What qualities does a person need to be a good president of the United States?
   _____
   _____

5. What if no one was allowed to get married until age 30?
   _____
   _____

POWER PLAY

How could brainstorming with members of your family help plan a picnic or a party? How could brainstorming with friends help decide which video to rent? How could brainstorming with classmates help design a school flag?

LIGHTNING STRIKES

FS112114 POWERTHINK — Frank Schaffer Publications

Name(s)_____

GOOD IDEA

When you brainstorm, you write down all the ideas people have without being concerned if they are good or bad, useful or not. Once you have taken advantage of the combined brain power and thinking skills of the members of your group, you can go one step further. You can **evaluate** your ideas.

The topic our group discussed was: _____

_____

_____

Look back at the ideas you wrote (What If Green Was Illegal?) and talk about them one at a time. Give everyone a chance to express opinions. After discussing each idea, select the one the group feels will work best. If the group doesn't agree, take a vote.

The best idea we had was: _____

_____

_____

Work together to list reasons why your idea could work.

The reasons we think this idea would work are:

_____

_____

_____

_____

_____

POWER PLAY
Give ideas a chance before you turn them down. It could be that one which seems silly at first might be just what you need.

LIGHTNING STRIKES

34 Frank Schaffer Publications

FS112114 POWERTHINK

Name(s)_____

SCHOOL TWELVE MONTHS A YEAR

What if someone on the school board suggested holding school twelve months a year instead of nine? The school year would start the first Monday after New Year's and run until the third week in December. School would be closed for two weeks in March, June, and September for vacations.

Spend time thinking about both sides of the issue. Work with a partner. Discuss reasons for and against having school twelve months a year. List your ideas below.

Change school year to 12 months:

Leave school year as is:

POWER PLAY
How can looking at both sides of a question help you see both points of view? How could listing pros and cons help you solve a problem or make a decision?

LIGHTNING STRIKES

HELP WANTED

Bat Chaser
Person needed to chase bats out of the church bell tower. Must not be afraid of heights or bats. Previous experience necessary. Hours: 10 p.m. to 6 a.m., Friday and Saturday. Pay based on experience.

If you were in charge of writing a help-wanted ad, you would need to know as much about the job as possible. Talk with your partner about the personal characteristics needed to repair and sell used bicycles. Write your ideas below.

Skills _____

Knowledge _____

Interests _____

Work habits _____

Other characteristics _____

Using the knowledge and skills you listed, write a help-wanted ad for someone to repair and sell used bicycles.

Help Wanted:_____

_____

_____

_____

_____

POWER PLAY

How can thinking and talking about a topic help you understand it better?

Now try to write want ads for other things, like books, comic books or cartoon characters, toys or fantastic, futuristic bicycles.

Example: WANTED: Caped crime fighter. Should have muscles of steel and the ability to leap tall buildings in single bound. Immunity to Kryptonite helpful but not necessary. Some newspaper work required. Must be willing to wear the letter "S" on chest.

LIGHTNING STRIKES

Name(s)_____

SIDEWALK PLANNER

A new gymnasium has just been built on the school grounds. The architect has asked you to help her design sidewalks from the school building to the new gymnasium. As you think about the problem, keep these things in mind:

1. The gymnasium and the school building are separated by an open field, which the children use during recess.

2. A student must be able to leave the school buildings from any of the three exits and reach the gymnasium without ever having to leave the sidewalk.

3. The sidewalks do not have to be straight lines.

Draw the sidewalks in on this map to show where you think they should be placed.

POWER PLAY

Show your design to your partner. Together, answer these questions:

What are the advantages of your design?

What are some possible problems?

What are some possible ways to deal with the problem?

LIGHTNING STRIKES

FS112114 POWERTHINK

Frank Schaffer Publications

37

CIRCLE, RECTANGLE, OR TRIANGLE?

Look carefully at the numbers in the circles, rectangles, and triangles in the figure below.

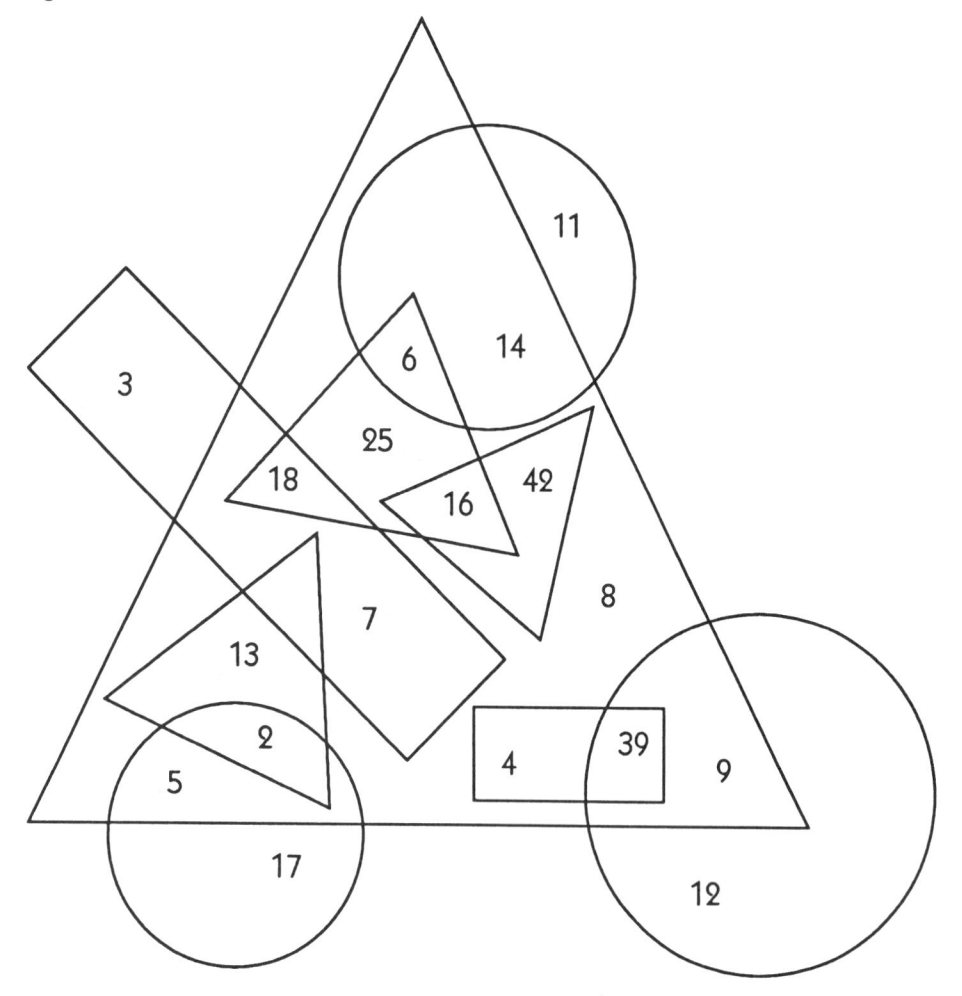

POWER PLAY
Make your own puzzle. Use circles, triangles, squares, rectangles, ovals, or any other shape you can name. Place numbers in different spots within your puzzle. Make a list of questions and exchange papers with your partner. How many answers can you find?

LIGHTNING STRIKES

1. Which numbers are in a rectangle, but not a circle? _3 & 7_

2. Which numbers are in a triangle and a circle? ~~~~ _6, 2_

3. Which numbers are in a triangle, but not in a circle or a rectangle?
   _16, 42_

4. Which numbers are in exactly two triangles, but not in a circle or rectangle? _16_

5. Which numbers are in a circle, but not a triangle? _9, 12_

38   Frank Schaffer Publications   FS112114 POWERTHINK

Name(s)_____

JOKERS AREN'T WILD

Learning the basics of adding and subtracting can be dull for young children. If you were teaching math to first and second graders, what kind of fun activities could you use to help them learn?

What about using a deck of cards without the jacks, queens, and kings? You could deal each person two cards and ask him or her to add the two together. You could give the person a chip for each right answer. You could pick a number (for example, 11) and every time the two cards added up to 11 the person could receive a bonus chip.

Work with a small group to think of some ideas for making learning math fun. Explain your ideas and what age group they would be appropriate for.

Use common, everyday objects, rather than fancy gadgets. Some examples you could use would be a pair of dice, small stones, marbles, chips, jelly beans, or cards.

Fun ideas for teaching math:

POWER PLAY
Making a game of learning can be fun for teachers and students.

LIGHTNING STRIKES

FS112114 POWERTHINK

Frank Schaffer Publications

Name(s)_____

NUMBER SLEUTH

Each of the four shapes contains 20 three-digit numbers, but only three of them can be found in all four shapes. What are the three numbers?

Talk with your partner about different ways to work this problem. List some different ways.

_____
_____

Put a star in front of the method you both decide to use.

Explain why you decided to use that method.

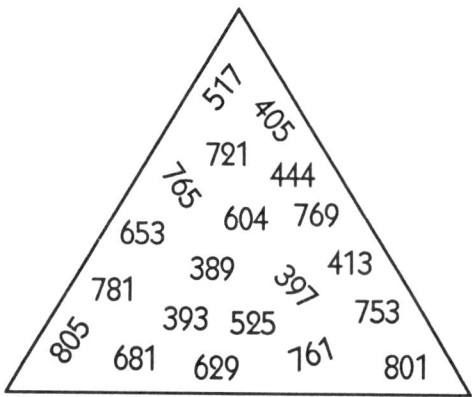

_____
_____

POWER PLAY

As a practical joke, three fifth graders managed to sneak into the fourth-grade and sixth-grade class pictures. (They are also in the fifth grade picture.) Describe how you would figure out who the three students were.

Triangle: 517, 405, 721, 444, 765, 604, 769, 653, 389, 413, 781, 397, 393, 525, 753, 805, 681, 629, 761, 801

Rectangle (tall): 549, 604, 357, 222, 493, 665, 793, 697, 717, 761, 709, 729, 777, 505, 589, 397, 733, 685, 449, 349

Square: 553, 469, 365, 417, 385, 561, 761, 604, 817, 477, 669, 597, 545, 457, 361, 888, 397, 601, 749, 673

Circle: 453, 785, 465, 541, 604, 373, 789, 821, 242, 489, 809, 661, 337, 761, 612, 116, 397, 485, 369, 713

LIGHTNING STRIKES

What three numbers did you find in all four shapes?

_____

40 Frank Schaffer Publications
FS112114 POWERTHINK

BEST BUY?

POWERTHINKING can help you and your family when you go grocery shopping. You look at the price of two different brands of corn. Both are 16-ounce cans. If one brand sells for $.59 and another brand sells for $.69, it's simple to figure out which is the better buy. But it's not always easy to tell which item is the best buy at first glance. Many grocery items come in various sizes and strengths.

Now you're in the health and beauty aisle. Two brands of cold tablets are available. One brand sells for $2.99 and the other sells for $3.99. Both packages contain 10 tablets. At first the package for $2.99 seems better. Then you read the back of the package. The brand for $2.99 says take two tablets every four hours. The more expensive brand says take one tablet every six hours.

Now which is a better buy? Work with a partner to find out.

Consider the tablets for $2.99 first, then the ones for $3.99.

Talk with your partner about each step needed to figure out which brand of cold tablet is the best buy. List the steps here.

_____
_____
_____
_____

Which package of cold tablets is the best buy? _____

Explain your answer. _____
_____
_____
_____

POWER PLAY

The best buy isn't always obvious. Can you think of other situations in a grocery store where you could use your math and POWERTHINKING skills?

With a partner, list reasons why a can of corn that sells for $.59 might not be a better buy than a same size can that sells for $.69.

LIGHTNING STRIKES

Name(s)_____

MISSING PIECES

Have you ever tried to put a jigsaw puzzle or a model together and found you were missing some pieces? That can be very frustrating.

Completing a sequence with missing numbers can also be difficult, but don't give up. The numbers aren't lost forever. With a little persistence, you can find them.

Here's a simple one to get you started.

2 4 6 ___ 10 ___ 14 16 ___ 20 ___

Since the numbers increase by 2 each time, you would fill in 8, 12, 18, and 22.

KILOWATT LEVEL
Work with a partner to fill in the missing numbers or shapes in each row. Talking about how the sequence is arranged can help solve the problem.

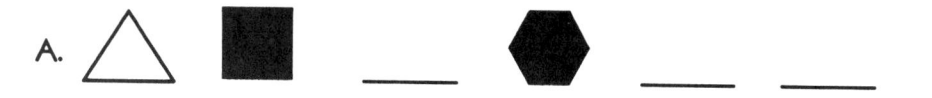

A. △ ■ ___ ⬣ ___ ___

B. 1 1 2 3 ___ 8 ___ 21 ___ ___

C. (triangle B-A-C) (triangle A-C-B) ___ ___ (triangle A-C-B)

D. 2 6 18 ___ ___ ___ ___ ___ 39,366

E. 31 28 31 ___ 31 ___ 31 31 ___ ___ ___

F. 1600 800 ___ ___ 100 ___ 25 ___ 6.25

G. 1 2 4 7 11 ___ ___ ___ ___ ___ 67

MEGAWATT LEVEL
Finish this sequence:

H. O T T F F S ___ ___ ___ ___ T

POWER PLAY
With your partner, make up a sequence. Use colors, shapes, numbers, or letters. After you have written the sequence, exchange papers with another group of students. Try to figure out the sequence you have been given.

LIGHTNING STRIKES

42

Frank Schaffer Publications

FS112114 POWERTHINK

Name(s)_____

TOO GOOD TO BE TRUE?

Every year since 1984, the teacher of the fifth-grade class at Elmgrove Elementary has counted and recorded the total number of cavities in the class. In 1992, the Whiteness Toothpaste Company provided the class with a free supply of toothpaste. The company then used the 1992 cavity count in a newspaper advertisement. Study this chart and read the advertisement underneath.

Year	Total number of cavities in the fifth-grade class
1984	17
1985	26
1986	19
1987	27
1988	18
1989	25
1990	17
1991	28
1992	18

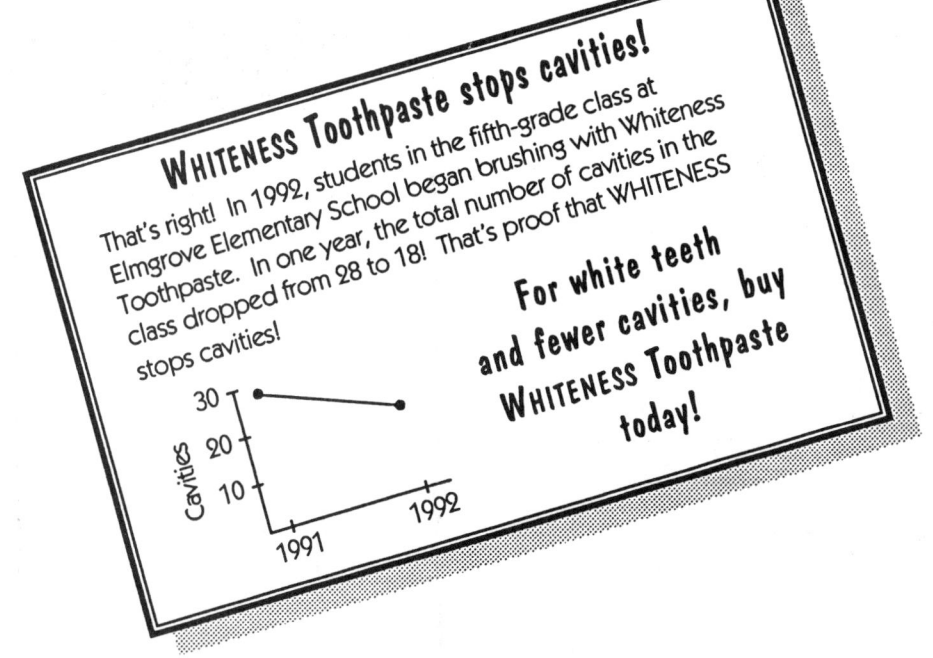

WHITENESS Toothpaste stops cavities!

That's right! In 1992, students in the fifth-grade class at Elmgrove Elementary School began brushing with Whiteness Toothpaste. In one year, the total number of cavities in the class dropped from 28 to 18! That's proof that WHITENESS stops cavities!

For white teeth and fewer cavities, buy WHITENESS Toothpaste today!

Draw a line graph showing the total number of cavities in the fifth-grade class from 1984 to 1992.

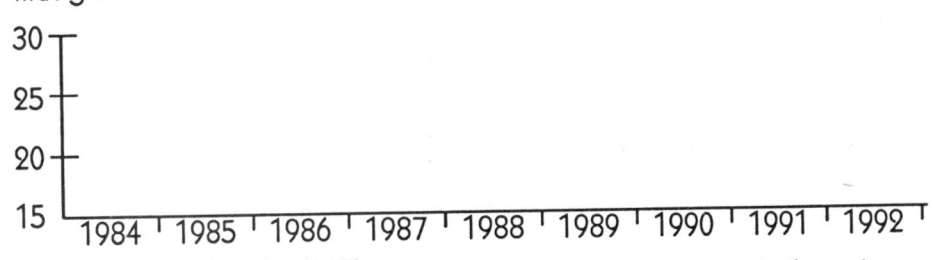

Go on to the next page.

LIGHTNING STRIKES

FS112114 POWERTHINK

Frank Schaffer Publications

43

Name(s)_____

TOO GOOD TO BE TRUE?

Answer the questions:

1. What information did the advertisement leave out?

   _____
   _____
   _____
   _____

2. Why do you think the Whiteness Company left out that information?

   _____
   _____
   _____
   _____

3. Is the line graph in the ad misleading? Why or why not?

   _____
   _____
   _____
   _____

POWER PLAY
With a partner, use the line graph you made to make your own advertisement in which you respond to the Whiteness Toothpaste Company.

LIGHTNING STRIKES

44
Frank Schaffer Publications

FS112114 POWERTHINK

Name(s) _____

WHAT THE WORLD REALLY NEEDS IS...

Are you a person who daydreams about impossible things? Someone who says, "What we really need is water that we can breathe," or "Why doesn't someone find a way to make rain and snow land only on lawns and gardens and fields and not on streets and sidewalks?" or "Wouldn't it be great to travel anywhere on Earth instantly?"

Or are you a person who says, "That's a crazy idea. It will never work." That's what some people told the Wright brothers about the airplane. Many people didn't believe Thomas Edison's light bulb or phonograph would ever work.

The world needs dreamers, people who aren't afraid to say "What if..." and then try to do something to make their dreams come true.

Work with a partner to think of inventions the world really needs, such as things we don't have or a new, better way of doing something. Think out loud. Be silly. Be imaginative.

Write a brief description of one of your ideas for a new invention.

POWER PLAY

How can being open to new ideas help you become a better POWERTHINKER?

With a partner, imagine that we could travel anywhere in the world instantly. Make a list of at least 100 things that would become unnecessary. After making up the list, decide with your partner whether or not you would favor instant-travel research. Explain your reasons.

What the world really needs is.... _____
_____

How would it work? _____
_____

What unexpected problems could it cause? _____
_____

How could you deal with these problems? _____
_____
_____

Why do we need it? _____
_____

How would it make life easier or better? _____
_____
_____

Who would use it? _____
_____

LIGHTNING STRIKES

Name(s)_____

THIS IS NOT A TEST

In science you've learned many exciting and interesting things about plants and animals, your body and how it works, weather, astronomy, rocks and minerals, volcanoes, gravity, and oceans.

What area of science is your class studying now? Think about some of the things you've learned. Work with a partner to write five questions that could be used on a science test.

If you were studying about weather, you might ask, "Why do we hear thunder after we see lightning?" or "How is wind speed measured?"

1. _____
2. _____
3. _____
4. _____
5. _____

Now think again about what you're studying in science. Write down some questions about the subject that you would like to have answered.

If the subject is weather, you might ask, "Why does thunder last longer than lightning?" or "How does a thermometer work?"

List questions about your subject.

_____
_____
_____
_____

POWER PLAY
Figure out a way to answer at least one of your questions, and answer it!

LIGHTNING STRIKES

Name(s) _____

WHY DO ZEBRAS HAVE STRIPES?

Imagine you have a research paper due for science class next week. Where do you begin?

First, you need to decide on the topic.

Think about areas that interest you. Write some questions you might be interested in finding answers to.

- How are hurricanes formed?
- How does the human brain work?
- How are amphibians different from reptiles?
- What's the difference between red and white blood cells?
- Why do leaves change color in fall?

Write some questions that could be used as possible topics for a science paper.

_____
_____
_____
_____
_____

Select the question you like best and underline it.

- How is a rainbow formed?
- How far away are the stars?
- Why does the sun appear yellow?
- Why does the water look blue?

POWER PLAY
Why are questions a good place to start?

LIGHTNING STRIKES

Name(s)_____

MORE QUESTIONS

In the activity, "Why Do Zebras Have Stripes?", you listed questions to help you decide on a topic for a science report.

Write the question that you underlined: _____

_____

Before you run off to the library, ask yourself some questions about your question.

If your question was "How are hurricanes formed?" you might list additional questions like, "Where are they formed? What time of year do they occur? What happens when a hurricane strikes land? How does a hurricane end?"

List more questions on your topic.

_____
_____
_____
_____

Finally, ask yourself these questions. Some ideas are listed. Add more of your own.

What types of sources will help me find answers to my questions?
    Atlas, encyclopedia...

What kinds of people could I write to or ask to find out more information?
    Scientists...

What can I do to learn more about the topic through observation or experimenting?
    Watch a video....

POWER PLAY
How does asking questions help you organize a project?

LIGHTNING STRIKES

48 Frank Schaffer Publications

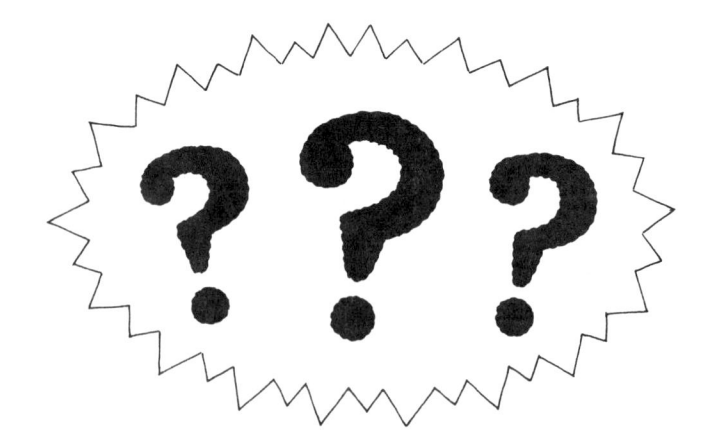

FS112114 POWERTHINK

Name(s)_____

A ROBOT FOR YOU

Computer chips aren't found only in computers. Telephones, televisions, washers and dryers, microwave ovens, digital watches, cars, and even some grocery store check-outs contain computer chips. Some types of computer chips store information or instructions. Video games use this type. Some chips process information. This type is found in computers and calculators.

You and your classmates are part of a "think tank" for a company developing a robot companion for children between the ages of 6 and 18.

Work with a small group. List what you think the new companion robot should be able to do. How would it look? What special attachments should it have?

The robot companion should be able to perform these functions:	The robot companion should have these attachments and should look like this:

POWER PLAY

With a partner, list products that we use today that weren't even invented 100 years ago. Then list some ways that you think life will be different 100 years from now.

LIGHTNING STRIKES

Name(s) _____

INTERPLANETARY MESSAGE

You have been asked to design a message that will be carried into space on an interplanetary probe. The message should send friendly greetings from Planet Earth, and be understandable to any intelligent life forms that might run across the probe. The message will be carried on a gold-plated plaque.

Work with a partner to write and design the message. To help you think about the project, answer these questions:

1. How will you make the message understandable to life forms that do not understand any languages spoken on Earth?
   _____
   _____

2. What diagrams or pictures could you use?
   _____
   _____

3. What will you tell the extraterrestrials about Earth? What *won't* you tell them?
   _____
   _____

4. Will the message include an invitation to visit Earth?
   _____

Design your message in the rectangle below:

POWER PLAY

Pretend that you are that extraterrestrial that received a message sent from Earth. What words or pictures in your message would you not be able to understand if you had no prior knowledge of Earth? Discuss with your partner how you might change your message to make it more easily understood by someone (or something) from another planet.

LIGHTNING STRIKES

50 Frank Schaffer Publications
FS112114 POWERTHINK

Name(s)_____

THE SHADOW KNOWS

Study the shadow picture in the middle of the page. Look closely at details. Can you find the drawing that is exactly the same as the shadow?

POWER PLAY

Sometimes we must look closely to see the differences between objects. Attention to detail is important in many occupations.

Talk with your partner about the methods you used to find the matching elephant. How were your elephant-finding methods alike? How were they different?

LIGHTNING STRIKES

I looked for how the tusks were shaped how the feet were aligned what shape the tail was how the body was and how the trunk was shaped.

FS112114 POWERTHINK

Frank Schaffer Publications

51

Name(s)_____

CREATING NEW COLORS

For this activity you will need paints and popsicle sticks or toothpicks.

If you mix one drop of blue paint with an equal amount of yellow paint, what color would you get?

You probably know from experience that you would get green.

But what if you mixed one drop of blue and two drops of yellow? Or three drops of yellow?

What about mixing red and brown? Orange and purple?

Use clean popsicle sticks or toothpicks to place drops of paint in the squares below. Think about what color you'll create. Record which colors you used, then mix the paint in each square with a clean toothpick. What color did you end up with? Is that what you expected? Were you surprised?

I mixed
___ drops of _____
___ drops of _____
___ drops of _____

I thought my new color would be _____
My new color actually is _____

I mixed
___ drops of _____
___ drops of _____
___ drops of _____

I thought my new color would be _____
My new color actually is _____

I mixed
___ drops of _____
___ drops of _____
___ drops of _____

I thought my new color would be _____
My new color actually is _____

POWER PLAY

When you created your colors, you wrote down how many drops of each color you used.

Exchange papers with your partner. Try to follow your partner's recipe for a new color. How did it work? Did you end up with the same color? Why or why not?

LIGHTNING STRIKES

Frank Schaffer Publications

FS112114 POWERTHINK

Name(s) _____

REASONS TO CELEBRATE

For this activity you may need crayons, markers or colored pencils, colored paper, scissors, tape, glue, and a stapler.

With the supplies listed above, make some holiday decorations.

Before you start cutting out pumpkins, Christmas trees, Easter eggs, or pilgrims, read on. . . . There's a catch.

First you have to make up the holiday. Any days already celebrated as national holidays are out.

What do you want to celebrate? You could use someone's birthday (even your own birthday) or make up a national holiday you think we should have, like National Pizza Day, National Walrus Watching Day, or National Wear a Sock on Your Head Day.

What's the name of your holiday?
National Art day

When should it be celebrated?
April 7th

Why did you pick that date? because that is the same day of my friends birthday and she loves art.

Why should people celebrate your holiday? because art is fun to do and you can't have a wrong picture

What type of decorations are appropriate for your holiday?
paintings everywhere, streamers, cakes with different designs on them

What can people do with your decorations? (Hang them from the ceiling? Display them in the window? Wear them?)
they can display different art inside their window, they can make art pins to wear

Go ahead and make your decorations. Have fun.

POWER PLAY
Of the holidays we celebrate, which one is your favorite? Imagine that we were tired of celebrating it the same old way. How would you change the holiday to make it more exciting?

LIGHTNING STRIKES

Halloween. To change Halloween you could go to different theme parks all over the world and not pay an admission and everything would be free. We could make a special type of candy that everybody passes out that lets you eat it in 1 night and not get sick

Name(s)_____

A LETTER WITHOUT WORDS

Write a letter using as few words as possible. Instead of words, use pictures. You could use a picture of a deer for the word dear, of a bee for be, and of an eye for I. How could you write "I saw birds fly South."?

Work with a partner to write your letter. Try to use more pictures than words.

POWER PLAY

With your partner, make a list of words for which pictures can be substituted. Use as many of them as you can to write a short story together.

LIGHTNING STRIKES

Yours truly,

54 Frank Schaffer Publications

FS112114 POWERTHINK

Name(s)_____

WHAT'S THE PROBLEM?

A problem is a difficult situation that needs to be worked out. To solve a problem you need to find an answer. Everyone has problems. What if you opened your lunch bag and found something weird inside? Would that be a problem?

What if you lost your math book? What if your older sister dumped ice water on you whenever you fell asleep?

You can solve many problems on your own. Don't give up if you can't find a solution right away. Use your **POWERTHINKING** skills to evaluate problems and find solutions.

Work with a partner. Talk about your ideas as you go through the steps to solve a problem.

You can't solve a problem if you don't know what the problem is to begin with, so...

STEP 1: State the problem.
Your parents are working late today. Your older brother is at basketball practice and your sister is taking bagpipe lessons. It's your turn to make supper and you don't know what to make.

The problem is: _____

Now that you know the problem is what to make for supper, you can go on to the next step.

STEP 2: List possible choices.
Don't limit yourself to the obvious. Be different. Think of some unusual choices. Perhaps baked liver topped with spinach?

List at least three possible choices, more if you wish.

1. _____
2. _____
3. _____

POWER PLAY
Stating a problem is the first step to solving it. Looking at possible alternatives is the second step. Talk with your partner about how you apply these steps to other situations. What should you do for your science project? You have a book report due. What book should you read?

LIGHTNING STRIKES

FS112114 POWERTHINK

Frank Schaffer Publications

Name(s)_____

WHAT NEXT?

Now that you know what the problem is and you have listed your choices, go on to the next step.

STEP 3:

List the pros and cons (good and bad points) for each choice.

Choice: Baked liver topped with spinach.

Pros	**Cons**
Very healthful	You don't like liver or spinach
Dad likes liver	You can't find a recipe
Mom likes spinach	Your brother won't eat liver
	Your sister thinks spinach is yucky

Write the pros and cons for at least three of the options you listed.

Option 1: _____

Pros   **Cons**

_____   _____
_____   _____
_____   _____

Option 2: _____

Pros   **Cons**

_____   _____
_____   _____
_____   _____

Option 3: _____

Pros   **Cons**

_____   _____
_____   _____
_____   _____

If you listed more than three options or need more space to write your pros and cons, use the back of this page or another sheet of paper.

POWER PLAY

How does looking at the pros and cons of each option help in problem solving? Would this work if your problem was what project to do for the Science Fair?

LIGHTNING STRIKES

Frank Schaffer Publications

FS112114 POWERTHINK

CONSIDER YOUR CHOICES

You've stated the problem, listed your choices and the pros and cons for each. Now what?

STEP 4:
Compare the pros and cons

Go back and look at the pros and cons you wrote. Give each of the pros and cons a weight between 1 and 10. The more important the pro or con, the more it should "weigh." Eliminate the choices where the cons outweigh the pros. This doesn't mean that you should eliminate all choices that have more cons than pros. (One powerful pro can outweigh ten weak cons.) Compare instead the total "weight" of the pros and cons.

Which choices did you eliminate? _____
_____
_____

Finally, you have arrived at...

STEP 5:
Select the best choice from the ones left.

What did you decide to make for supper? _____

Why did you make that decision? _____
_____

REVIEW:
The five steps for solving a problem are:
1. State the problem.
2. List possible solutions or choices.
3. List pros and cons for each choice.
4. Weigh the pros and cons.
5. Select one of your choices.

List other problems you could work out using these five steps.
_____
_____
_____
_____

POWER PLAY
By using these steps, many problems can be broken down and solved.

With a partner, choose one of the problems you listed. Solve it together using the five steps you just learned.

LIGHTNING STRIKES

Name(s)_____

WHAT WOULD YOU DO?

Have you ever been faced with a problem and not known what to say or do? It happens to everybody.

Should you be truthful? Should you be nice? Should you close your eyes and wish you were on another planet?

Select one of the situations listed below. Work through the five steps for solving a problem with your partner. Use the next page to work through the problem.

- You and Gwen are shopping for new clothes. She tries on an outfit she really likes. The color looks terrible on her. She asks you what you think.

- Stan invites you to stay for supper and try his special secret spaghetti sauce. He spent hours making it. You take one taste and think it's terrible.

- Your uncle gave you a six-foot purple, plastic armadillo for your birthday. You were hoping for a new wallet.

- You saw your best friend put a candy bar in his pocket without paying for it.

THE FIVE STEPS FOR SOLVING A PROBLEM ARE:
State the problem.
List possible solutions or choices.
List pros and cons for each choice.
Weigh the pros and cons.
Select one of the choices.

WHAT WOULD YOU DO?

Name(s)_____

1. State the problem:_____
2. List possible solutions or choices:

    (a.) _____ (b.) _____ (c.) _____

3. List pros and cons for each choice:
4. Give each pro and con a weight between 1 and 10 and total the weights of all pros and cons.

Pros and Cons:

Pros	Weight	Cons	Weight
(a.) _____	_____	_____	_____
_____	_____	_____	_____
_____	_____	_____	_____
Total	_____	Total	_____
(b.) _____	_____	_____	_____
_____	_____	_____	_____
_____	_____	_____	_____
Total	_____	Total	_____
(c.) _____	_____	_____	_____
_____	_____	_____	_____
_____	_____	_____	_____
Total	_____	Total	_____

POWER PLAY
Select one of the solutions and explain your choice.

LIGHTNING STRIKES

FS112114 POWERTHINK — Frank Schaffer Publications

Name(s)_____

A PLAN FOR YOUR FUTURE

A goal is something you want to accomplish. Setting goals can help you map out a plan. If you don't know where you're going, how will you know when you get there?

Short term goals cover things you want to do today or in the next week or so. Examples: pass your geography test next Tuesday or improve your batting average in Friday's game.

Long term goals are things you want to achieve in the next year or longer, like graduating from high school or attending college.

Your goals don't have to be easy, but they should be **realistic**. Is a goal to grow nine inches taller by next week realistic?

Once you have determined what goals you want to accomplish, you can set up a plan to reach those goals.

To pass your geography test you could plan to study a certain amount of time on Sunday and Monday. To improve your batting average, you could practice every day before the game.

POWER PLAY

Setting goals and making plans on how to reach those goals are like using a map to get to a new place. You may decide to change your route along the way. You may even change your mind about where you are going. But if you didn't have a goal in mind at the beginning, how would you ever get started?

LIGHTNING STRIKES

List a goal for today.   How can you reach that goal?

List a goal for one month from today.   How can you reach that goal?

List a goal you would like to reach one year from now.   How can you reach that goal?

What goal would you like to reach by the time you are 20?   How can you reach that goal?

Name(s)_____

RECOGNIZING FEELINGS

Some feelings are considered "good" because they make people feel good. List some types of feelings that make you feel good.

_____

_____

Some feelings are considered "bad" because they make people unhappy. List some types of feelings that make you feel bad.

_____

_____

Think about each of the "bad" feelings listed below. Define it by giving an example.

Sad is how I feel when <u>my favorite baseball team loses.</u>

Grief is what I feel when _____

_____

I feel **lonely** when _____

_____

I feel **afraid** when _____

_____

I feel **disappointed** when _____

_____

I feel **frustrated** when _____

_____

I feel **rejected** when _____

_____

I feel **jealous** when _____

_____

POWER PLAY
When we have a "bad" feeling, we can look at the cause. Sometimes understanding the reason for the feeling helps us deal with it better.

LIGHTNING STRIKES

ENCOURAGING POWERTHINKING

One of the additional benefits of teaching critical thinking and problem solving in your classroom is that it is an excellent forum for positive reinforcement. Try some of these on for size!

That's an excellent question.

Perhaps that idea would work. Let's try it.

That's a creative way of looking at it.

Not many people would have come up with such an unusual idea.

Terrific idea!

Very interesting thought! Maybe it would work.

I never thought of it that way. Good idea!

That could be just the ticket!

That suggestion makes a lot of sense.

That idea is pretty fantastic.

What a wonderful thought!

That suggestion is quite unique.

That shows you're really thinking.

Let's consider Joe's idea.

Very imaginative!

Splendid!

What a marvelous plan!

Let's consider Sue's recommendation.

Very creative!

Let's give Kim a round of applause for that suggestion.

Very inventive!

Let's follow Tim's line of thinking and see where it goes.

Now why didn't I think of that? Good job.

How did you ever think of such a good idea?

Congratulations on coming up with that solution.

You're very observant!

Your good ideas are popping like popcorn.

That could be just the answer we need.

All right!

That idea shows you're really thinking.

You're quite a **POWERTHINKER.**

Your question shows you put a lot of thought into the problem.

You're really thinking today!

Good going!

That's a pretty awesome idea!

Brilliant idea!

You're very creative.

Great plan!

I knew you could figure out an answer for yourself.

You handled that tough problem very well.

Wow! I'm impressed.

You made a wise decision.

You handled that problem well.

Brilliant!

Jill has the hang of it now.

What an interesting proposal!

This class is full of good ideas today.

See what you can accomplish!

Working together really works.

Well done!

I can't believe all the great ideas you've had today.

Nice job!

Keep up the good work.

That is so outrageous it's contagious!

BIBLIOGRAPHY

For Teachers:

Heiman, Marcia and Slomianko, Joshua. Critical Thinking Skills.
    Washington, DC: National Education Association, 1986.
Moore, Brooke Noel and Parker, Richard. Critical Thinking.
    Mountain View, CA: Mayfield Publishing Company, 1986.
Van Oech, Roger. A Kick in the Seat of the Pants.
    New York: Harper & Row, 1986.
Van Oech, Roger. A Whack on the Side of the Head.
    New York: Warner Books, 1990.
Cobb, Vicki. How to REALLY Fool Yourself: Illusions for All Your Senses.
    Philadelphia, PA: J.B. Lippincott, 1981.
Costa, Arthur A. Developing Minds: A Resource Book for Teaching Thinking, Volumes I and II.
    Washington, DC: Association for Supervision and Curriculum Development, 1991.
Curriculum Update. Washington, DC: Association for Supervision and Curriculum Development. June, 1993.

For Students:

Bendick, Jeanne. Observation.
    New York: Franklin Watts, Inc., 1972.
Berry, Joy. Every Kid's Guide to Handling Feelings.
    Chicago: Children's Press, 1986.
Berry, Joy. Every Kid's Guide to Thinking and Learning.
    Chicago: Children's Press, 1987.
Berry, Marilyn. Help Is on the Way For: Thinking Skills.
    Chicago: Children's Press, 1986.
Bernards, Neal. Advertising: Distinguishing Between Fact and Opinion.
    San Diego: Greenhaven Press, Inc., 1963.
Burns, Marilyn. The Book of Think (Or How to Solve a Problem Twice Your Size).
    Boston: Little, Brown and Company, 1976.
Cobb, Vicki. How to REALLY Fool Yourself: Illusions for All Your Senses.
    New York: J.B. Lippincott, 1981.
Gould, Laurence J. and William G. Martin. Think About It: Experiments in Psychology.
    Englewood Cliffs, NJ: Prentice-Hall, Inc.,1968.
Simon, Seymor. The Optical Illusion Book.
    New York: Four Winds Press, 1976.
Tchudi, Stephen. The Young Learner's Handbook.
    New York: Charles Scribner's Sons, 1987.

ANSWERS

page 9 — Carrots Make Your Ears Grow
1. C
2. C
3. N (a question)
4. C
5. C
6. N (a suggestion)
7. N (an order)
8. C
9. N (a question)
10. C

page 17 — What's the Connection?

Across
1. Continents
4. Hats
7. Birds
9. States
14. Oceans
17. Movies
18. Years
19. Trails
20. Dogs
21. Snakes

Down
1. Cities
2. Noises
3. Shapes
5. Toys
6. Rivers
8. Cats
10. Insects
11. Holidays
12. Pets
13. Candy
15. Sports
16. Months

page 38 — Circle, Rectangle, or Triangle?
1. 3, 18, 4, 7
2. 6, 14, 9, 2, 5
3. 8, 13, 25, 16, 42
4. 25, 42, 13
5. 17, 12, 11

page 40 — Number Sleuth
761, 397, and 604 appear in all four.

page 42 — Missing Pieces

A. (triangle, filled square, pentagon, filled hexagon, heptagon, filled octagon)

B. (1+1, 1+2, 2+3…) 1, 1, 2, 3, 5, 8, 13, 21, 34, 55

C. (five triangles with rotating A, B, C labels at vertices)

D. (×3) 2, 6, 18, 54, 162, 486, 1,458, 4,374, 13,122, 39,366
E. The numbers are the number of days in each month from January through December (except leap years when February has 29 days). 31, 28, 31, 30, 31, 30, 31, 31, 30, 31, 30, 31
F. (÷2) 1600, 800, 400, 200, 100, 50, 25, 12.5, 6.25
G. (+1+2+3…) 1, 2, 4, 7, 11, 16, 22, 29, 37, 46, 56, 67
H. The letters are the first letters of numbers beginning with one. Missing are S, E, N, T, E